emily & elsp...

Dagger Editions, an imprint of Caitlin Press Inc.
3375 Ponderosa Way
Qualicum Beach, BC V9K 2J8
www.daggereditions.com

Text design by Vici Johnstone
Cover design by Diane McIntosh
Cover art by RoseAnn Janzen

Printed in Canada

Caitlin Press Inc. acknowledges financial support from the Government of Canada and the Canada Council for the Arts, and the Province of British Columbia through the British Columbia Arts Council and the Book Publisher's Tax Credit.

Canada Council   Conseil des Arts   BRITISH COLUMBIA   Funded by the   Canada
for the Arts   du Canada   ARTS COUNCIL   Government
                                                           of Canada

Title: Emily & Elspeth / Catherine McNeil.
Other titles: Emily and Elspeth
Names: McNeil, Catherine, author.
Description: Poems.
Identifiers: Canadiana 20220215561 | ISBN 9781773860992 (softcover)
Classification: LCC PS8625.N4265 E45 2022 | DDC C811/.6—dc23

emily & elspeth

poems

catherine mcneil

Dagger Editions 2023

Contents

emily

before leaving the west coast

slipping away from herself   emily watches her body get up
salutes the sun   someone spies on her
                    has rented the suite across the street

emily picks up the coffee pot
                        pours   summerspill
                            through the window
someone has turned on the sun
                               frigate birds hitchhike
on BC ferries

the mountain   in prayer   swallows the sky

rose petals   dust   the heath

pigeons
                like wings   speed to the finish
                writers are caught
                in her mind

this is my home emily
thinks   takes little bird notes   her hurried hand

cats wave   "oo la la" as she passes by   she sings to bones
      "fa la la la la la la la la"
      eats what falls out of the sky

when closing her eyes
tears fall   ever since her car accident

she cuts the tears in half   puts them in a jar

there is always a staying before a leaving

mechanical tin cans

emily watches ten channels simultaneously
turnips in her ears   she's blown

her reptilian circuits   her head moves her

"there is an app i've got and an actual
person answers and tells you what the weather is"

emily stares into a vast emptiness
a little lost   she can not breathe   she is nowhere

locating herself   cars high-tail

                pyrotechnics
            at English Bay
        blow herons from their nests
            emily cannot hear her self-

hypnosis tape   jabs in another shellac-laden sweetie
downs tea with maltitol   sorbitol
                anything at all at all

            feels like a feedlot everyone
tailgating

the herd   trapped in their mechanical tin cans

chewing   the ferrous taste of blood on emily's tongue

in the middle

emily's tires smack the pavement
she pulls off Highway 101
heading west in her wet purple Honda
she knows the etiquette

of the highway   drives in the middle   of the lane   squawks

at anything at all off centre   glances rearview for
        the man   with the cam   panning

        terrified of cars flying around her   she's been hit
more times than she can count

her car lifts off as her right front tire hits roadkill   *shit*
probably a cat   they'd be better off at home   declawed
fur and feathers   under tired tires   birds   pigeons   squirrels
how many has she buried this year?

the driver in front of her put on the drag   emily honks

she loves her horn   car ahead screeches to a halt
            churlish yellowbeard climbs out
marches towards her   bellowing   shaking fist

emily rolls up her window   puts her car in reverse   taps
the vehicle behind her

blackbeard climbs out as she drives away

shaking

brakes. against

emily was brought up in the Cascades
where mountain women jammed "up on rocky top"
drank from a nearby stream

now she flaps her wings
head down   opens her joyful window

in the west end   her right temporal lobe all set
                              to go go

everyone below her balcony familiar to her   she braces against the
sound of a semi shooting up Barclay

brrr   floats

above her street   is deposited back within her three walls
her house tells her what to do   bladder of the sky

        breaks open   frogs smack

the telegenic delivery girl   head shaped like a speaker phone
skateboarding down Barclay

sizzling pizza in a box   melts
her left paw   emily wakes

her right hand
                a clawhammer

frozen   ever since the accident   her fist

curls under chin   the embryonic prayer   every night

she done me wrong song

holy holy holy lord god of power   emily's afraid to cross
                             the Georgia viaduct
holy holy lord god of might
god abandons the gephyrophobe

should have known someone was travelling
the wrong road before emily smushed her   not this again

turns out she's cute   single   ready   to get naked   blessed are
those who come in the name of the lord   by their fruits

you will know them   so godsure   draw down the light
eat it   breathe it   dream it   halfway home   laughter

bounces off her hair   like sunshine   skipping over

emily sees her naked from behind

don't rush into her   eat out of her hands   back up before she
asks you to   one quick taste of the moon   at the edge of eyes

one leg up   one leg down   pinning her arms   lips
sense the honey   cold sore   breast reduction   taboob   always
in the dark   "you

have a good body"   like an afterthought   put herself together
quick pick

another reality
                   here emily loses story   backtracks   backs up
leaves the heart behind   such heavy luggage   extra baggage tags

eyes burn into her head   her breath scissors across the page
open books learn to keep their mouths shut and sing to cows
keep your tongue inside your mouth mole in ground

where does she get off?   we all fall   husha husha
         her tongue down
some fop's throat   leaves emily cold

sorry if you thought it was more

up the drive

emily pops into Sweet C   grabs a tikka   gabbles at the cashier
hits Joe's (window rainbow flagging peace) for a cup of foosh
knocks balls around   flicks quarters in the jukebox "Crimson and
Clover" over and over   wants a girl who can cha-cha-cha

yaks with Joe about Portugal and never returning
like emily's Papa who knew he couldn't go back to the Isle o' Skye
he'd never leave a second time   stop   talk   shop   next door
to Octopus books   chats with Charles Watts about writers

spinning their wheels in the noisy everyday   passed bearded
folk   the dyke crew cut barber   across to the park chow
down Cambozola from La Grotta Del Formaggio   panettone
from Carmelo's   above the traffic   always the djembe beat

a car jammed into Highlife's front window   outside Vancity
a woman emerges shaved head   chin stubble   sixty years   soiled dress
her mouth opening   closing   hand out   for a cigarette   emily knows
her well   "cravin' eh?" buys her a pack

into Victor Sam's who straightens her out   thick chiro
practical fingers in the centre of her forehead   down her temples
five taps   five times and off for a string of dry crimson blood
sausage hanging in rows in the window beside the Royal Bank

i could get fat living here she thinks chomping away   checking
out the cds in Tai's rip off pawn shop   blasting home for a siesta
before the talk of the town   Ivan Coyote & Rae Spoon's
"The Trucker's Memorial" have Lime bursting at the rafters

faster than dark

emily dreams two fires break out   her heat's jacked up
the cellar afire
violet flames skyrocket out of the fireplace

fires haunt her

like the sequoia they reseed

in the car objects are closer than they appear
she senses a camera filming

driving down Barclay   the road begins to

bisect

she pulls over   is this
how her eyes

have decided to age? could she hang up her eyelids

use those in the back
                              of her head?   keys go missing

  back inside the house   letters
                                      on recipe cards separate

whatever's in the fridge plopped into the pot of crock   water
cabbage onions carrots tomatoes key lime leaves lemongrass
corn pasta   she tastes the soup

to listen to it   lays down   light grows faster than dark
pats Isis
the now diseased cat whose claw drew blood
with a glove on

code of no go

emily eschews her father's code of "no   go   don't
make folk uncomfortable"

friars and elms   at Guardian Angel   seven o'clock mass
in waiting   waving

   the hurdy gurdy dad-voice

       "you may never live in a house again
       you're shouting so loud, i can't hear you"

folding in   two winks   under the falling gaze of this
humming
   poly-eyed town
       old lumpy-dumpy lazy luminous cloud
       moving backwards through *ochre time*

downtown someone sprinkles the happy spotted
bell flowers chirp

      "drinking   dripping   dirty dancing
      a glorious hallelujah to be sure
      oh how they woo ya
      let us give thanks"

into the silence of this morning she sees Christ's face
as she climbs Davie Street

each tap tap tap   her nails foreign
belong to someone else's body

orthotics   magnets   maryjanes

energy   force   feet   first

this new emily
some days   she sees good

the visible

emily scratches a cicatrix below her belly where her uterus was

she remembers her father chuntering in Latin and
her mother begging off after finishing her sentences
the registers of the letters move

her store-bought cat, the stormy petrel
knocks on the front door
what shall she do with the visible?

phoenix's ashes? the dead bird on her porch?
she extracts her fingers from her mouth

dreams at her doorstep
lie there dying

climbs out of the piano box she roosts in
the air moves fast but
reality protects itself

no one pokes wires through her scalp
skunks sprint across Robson
students do not disappear into Vancouver traffic
Coast Mountain doesn't smush a boy on Pender Street

emily feathers the lightness of bird into hand shovel
rides the elevator with her store-bought cat
deposits the bird below a bush

back inside lays down on her bed
faces appear, lovers

one walks
into the room

let us give thanks

freddy her faghag crush sexes her way into emily's room
born the day
lightning struck the water tower

the sun bedazzles   the rain

metallic star bodies   bump
  into the moon

the west end   blackberry   happy   sultry people   cheer

on horseback   goodness   would surely follow her

all of her days
when she passes   "Ou la la!"
                              she can see into your head

let us give thanks   in the dream she's left her husband
emily parents her girls

        for crying in the cock-eyed sink
        emily has loved   her

far too long   earth opens up   her foot falls in

        highway to the danger zone

starts to sink

            in

                sin

                    sing

lalalalala glor ia

cameras roll every which way
chickadees and robins tap   tap   tap their toes
to emily's broken banjo blues

tra la la   songs spring like exotic hot house flowers
emily slides
out of the frame   pats her numb plum tum   tulips hoist
up their red skirts

emily loved to run as a child   bounces
around in sneakers   freckles fly off her face   fa la la

hops past Barclay Market   turnips rock
belly slappin'   toe tappin'
finger snappin'   hand clappin'
claphappy   cha cha cha

ribbons of light grow closer to the place
she knows as her

further from fatigue and fibrositis

man with the cam in a red sedan

when emily pulls into the Safeway parking lot on Davie
she sees a man in a red sedan with John Lennon sunglasses
hair spiking out from below a ball cap
pull in and park a few spots behind her

she slings her baby taylor and ukulele over her right shoulder
her accordian in its suitcase in her left   remembers
Delta Dawn with her suitcase and guitar in hand
she is a poet and a one woman band

she saunters to the bandstand in Alexandria Park
where she has a half hour slot this evening
laying on her blanket   again she espies this fellow
pointing a matchbox at her again

so she watches   does he light a cigarette? no
could it be him? yes a PI hired by Great West Life
trying to catch her functioning in the world
enjoying a moment of happiness

disabled people need to be laying down
at home at all times   stuffing themselves silly
beached whale-like   couch bound
hypnotized by the tele vision   infinitely depressed

yes she loves her couch
like everyone she knows who has ME/CFS
"i'm not dead yet" she thinks on the stage

sings "ukulady and i'm red hot   i'm here to play for you
ukulady and i'm red hot   i'm here to play for you
i love to play all day long and if you like you can sing along
ukulady and i'm red hot   i'm here to play for you, oh yeah

i'm here to play for you"

"don't step on my shoelaces"

shoot into the light
the man with the cam takes footage of

emily singing to herself the lips moving
but nobody's home

fair weather ha
a mask the devil dons the sky
flares its nostrils the air awakens nose hairs and monday
is a nightmare

emily is an aphasic iconoclast
she wrote a little song by the time she got home
sat beneath her sadhappy lamp she forgot it something

about teaching catholic boys is a fulltime job
chunks out of one's cheek recorded

as a child she loved
to run with fingers crossed now
finally she can get the doctor to tell her the truth

"can you help me? there's something wrong
with my shoelaces" elderly woman limps towards her
points down at her feet one shoelace tied to the other

emily undoes and reties them white skies

lift over English Bay

flight

dreams the man with a cam is on the plane to San Miguel

      straps on her bra just to

          think   straight

the neighbour's casa aflame

robin's egg blue
                  sunflower yellow
                              tangerine blush
emily enjoys noise flowing over
the rufous brick wall

glass particles in   clears   greens   browns   the blues

      like those she sang about on Sometimes Island

jut out of concrete

double espressos herself

knocks about the house in her maryjanes

'get-a-lot-done get-a-lot-done-and-be-happy'

the cuckoo clock thinks she's two loco

        laughs

at her 'siéntete escúchame' rolling from her blabbing
                    babbling
                    parabling

hotwired brain

her wee neighbour Joaquin toots one note
        interminably
               out the window
emily "what did you do today?"

"my mother is coming from everywhere" he says

the world smiles

too much sun

la la la la la
la la la la la la la la

periwinkle jacaranda   cacti   dot   ursine hills   Araceili

scrubs the ring around the rosy
                                  with a brick
emily raises a hue on the phone

   "Happy Birthday Dad"

Araceili says   "my father wishes your father
                       a happy day
                       happy day padre "

   her deceased father points his toes at the poinsettias
                   five stories high

   eternal rest on his bed of cloud in the mansion of the moon
             the kingdom of Mictlān

sparrowchuckle   Joaquin's bobbing head   shifts
          on emily's turquoise terrace

atencion

firecrackers detonate above emily's casita
still she sleeps   downtown someone

sprinkles the happy spotted bell flowers
are dripping, dancing   where's that line

from? esta mañana   emily notices a bald
white man (*who can tell by looking that*

a man is white?) in a PT cruiser park on
the wrong side of Calle Salida a Celaya

the hard-of-hearing paperman with silver
tipped teeth strolls up to the car with a copy

of the local news "Atencion"

"o sole mio"

skeinery sky
        loose limbed emily   looks every   which way
eyelashes flutter like birds long legs pressed up against

        the sixteenth century dining table   head three quarters to the right
          elbow on the table

she thinks entry to this world should cost more than a grand
        she can't get settled
             tapes up the chairseat jabbing her thigh
             how to keep the world together
             ibis' handstand

Mexican bugsnuggle in her English-Spanish dictionary
        Araceili whistling takes the kettle off
           whistling

last night emily dreamt
             she was screaming
"don't step on my shoelaces" at god

when she awoke a melody lodged in her mind   ggfedcdcg

washes her face   she's felt dirty ever since the bull
bloodbath in the Gran Corrida last night

outside her window yellow shutters   a little man his
little guitara   white fungal patches below his eyes
gumgrowth o'er his teeth ring around the collar   plucks

"o sole mio" for her

she's in a new body   a band in a body   a glorious
hallelujah to be sure
until she remembers her father telling her she couldn't

solo   couldn't be the cantor in the church choir
somebody always telling her she can't cantor

      trying to corral her canter

like Jackie O

lateday shine on maguey cacti   the size of trees   Orion directly above
the moon full now   for three fattening days

feels the need to succeed with speed   racing her motor   dreams
she crashes her punchbuggy

voices of construction workers knocking down the casa across
the street in Spanish   outside her bedroom window at five a.m.

     firecrackers
                     emily hits the ground

like Jackie O jumping out the back of the Lincoln   or the children

tossed up by Chapo the bull   slamming faces in the dirt   little beings
held to the ground   hands on heads   the animal killing them

tears of the boy at the corrida make sense   always such dread and
impossibility of what she calls her life

switches the nightlight on   dreams up the fear   urinating   defecating
spewing blood like the lethally injected

she had once lived there

a bus slowly turns the corner
the paperman hops on the bus

chats   rides the bus ten feet   passes
the driver his daily news   this was

how it was every morning at the corner
of emily's street   a policía in pale blue nylon

short-sleeved shirt with walkie-talkie
and gun in a black leather

pouch under a palm tree   trunk two feet
in diameter   white paint at its base

the first time she saw all of the trees with
white paint at the base of their trunks was

in 1988 driving to Cuernavaca from
City   when she had her déjà vu about the yellow

house she had once lived in

Rivera

1.

letter from emily to Diego

close the windows
shut the curtains
amor trapped in your casa

Diego what did you ever give to Frida?

> fire in your bedroom
> ignites your kitchen
> all of Coyoacán
> streetlocked in fire

monstrous two-timing toad of the consulate
she says she will eat your legs in tomato sauce

every time
she dies a little more

is a fishhook in mouth
butterflied to board

iron handrail torso to abdomen
pulled out by a passer-by
body pieced together
in a plastic corset

sad-gypsy-tangled-hair
"you are ugly for Rivera"

with your hands on Frida
she trembles
her body an earthquake

cracks her
collapses her backbone
your tongue down   her sister's throat

2.

don't look at this Diego

Maria   great companion   constant
she never abandoned you

you swore you'd always be faithful

cuni
cuni
cuni
cuni
cuni

Diego hide your eyes
                    Don't look at this

            Maria is Mari is Mari macho is lesbian

3.

why wait?

Frida doesn't want to suffer anymore
nothing works   her hands
her feet

    what does she need you for?
the earth opens up   feels her gangrene foot fly off
misses the other to navigate

hands clumsy
unable to paint
mouth mute   (no one to talk to)

her soul   in a multi-coloured huipil
waits for Diego to set it free

kiss her sweet life goodbye
in the kingdom of Mictlán
                          why wait?

Quebrado

the first time emily swims at the Hotel Mina Real
the Fuller Brush salesgirls are having a ball
being crowned princesses and reinas for top sales

they line up in the toiletseatless   toiletpaperless bathroom
blue and red banners with gold lettering slung over their shoulders   tiaras
atop heads of bodies of all shapes   squeezed tight into cocktail
gowns   dressed for each other

lanky emily stands in line   her bikini pink with padded top   shorts 1920's style
red cowboy hat   lips rosy with Burt's Bees
a woman waddles out of a cubicle   her red high heel broken

and all afternoon a young Mexican waiter full of favours and questions
"te gustaría algo? jugo de Jamaica?"
"cuánto cuesta?" emily inquires
"es gratis"   he replies   later

"where is your house?"
"do you have children?"
"you have an esposo?"
"an espresso?"
"no un esposo?"
"cansada?"
"no Canada?"

finally he points to emily's ring   "yes" she lies   when she was in Martinique
Josef   a local married Martiniquais man   begged her to be his mistress
he would fly her to the island where she could have anything she wanted

yes she had a ring
the relentless waiter disappeared

corrida de toros

in the corrida   the drummer's son of five cannot stop
crying horses amble   pace   rip palms apart with their teeth
circle as far as ropes permit under overhot five o'clock sun
'til trumpets sound   clapping   begins matadors on horseback
wave a hearty hello   hats held high   gold-trimmed velvet
jackets match their saddles   they circle the ring

banderilleros swirl their pink capes over the soil   horses
sidestep   back up to the four corners of the ring   a man holds
up a white sign Chapo   massive black bull   all shoulders
little legs thunders into the ring   "Heh Heh"   his head moves
him   charges at the fluttering cape swirling along the ground
the crowd shouts "Olé!"

a girl matador in black pants   jacket   tie and white shirt
whoops   swings her cape   a powerful far-sending chest pass
the bull attacks   lifts her on his horned head and flips her
she screams   lands   jumps   runs   the bull pursues her   she hits
the dirt   hands over head   lying face down

emily now sees why the little boy was crying   she's on the edge
of her seat   banderilleros taunt with capes   yank on Chapo's
tail   drool trails from his mouth   a new matador on horseback
about fifteen   "Heh Heh Heh" Chapo after him   clouds of dirt
the horse jumps on all fours   on its hind legs   rearing

"Toros Toros" the horse's eyes track Chapo's   the matador
plunges a green and white banderilla into the bull's back
"Bravo" mad hurrahs   and another   hits bone   roars   four
harpoons dangle out of the Chapo's left side   three on
the right

blood runnels red red neck to toes   what a brave bull
emily thinks   a banderillero standing behind the wall turns
to her   blows warm air into his hands folded in prayer   Chapo
losing heart   urinates   defecates   faces the crowd   faces emily
the boy next to her chews his nails

Chapo falls to his knees   one last plea   "Wa ha" his massive
groan   doesn't want to move   knows it's a set up   tears run down
the sides of emily's nose   "Ah ha heh" Chapo struggles to his feet
throws his head left to right   to shake out the seven harpoons
his headdress green and white

"Ah ha heh" Chapo charges   is knifed in the neck   his giant head
moves up and down as he spews blood a meter   a man walks up
stabs another knife deep into his heart   Chapo falls to the ground
fervent hurrahs

the man chops off Chapo's exposed ear   horses with gold
headdresses march into the ring   wild howls   "Bravo" a chain
around Chapo's lifeless neck   hitched to the horses   pull Chapo
out of the ring on a rack

the president holds up his ear   the audience's loco   hats fly
down from rafters   the matador flashes his smile at heaven   waves
at the crowd   tosses hats   jackets back into stands   trumpets   the horn
of plenty

Elspeth

Vancouver to San Miguel

Equipoise. Treetops spin, spit vowels under the double-faced moon. Elspeth stays where her hands are, on the wheel, barreling down Highway One, singing a song to Canada. "Oh Canada -ah -ah" as she zips through White Rock, by the sign *Welcome to the USA*, past border guards with quick-scented shepherds, and into the Land of Freedom. State law requires a Canadian domicile. Past tulips in Tulalip, Saginaw, Chuck-a-nut Drive, the Korean War Memorial in Oregon, where rolls the Columbian river.

A hand in Grand Canyon, Elspeth steals chunks of white quartz she sees while peeing. Past Kanab, the greatest show on earth, the sun arches across the sky. Hoodoos, thin pillars of limestone, spires bulbous stepping through time recount five hundred and twenty-five million years of history. On the radio, "there are more refugees in Lebanon than any other country in the world." Past coral clouds, chocolate cliffs, bristle cone, trees, Umpqua Park, Calapooya Creek.

She talks to her niece Bessie that night from Ruby's Inn. "Hi Aunt Lizzy, my phone fell into the outhouse." She fished it out, five feet down into the feculence. Says she got it out, but it still stinks when she talks on it.

Elpseth is still trying to convince herself reality is perfect. Author of her suffering, she remembers when she sold frogs for fifty cents, tadpoles a penny. Grey shapes, Mesozoic shape shifters, are held captive by the horizon. That night, peering out on her frost-laden balcony, she thinks how nicely a drink would go down below the belt of Orion.

Her mouthguard pinches the skin in her cheeks, she gnaws the excess skin as she climbs out from beneath the four hundred thread count sheets. She trips down the corridor to the washroom, pulls her shoulders back, points her shoulder blades together like angel wings. These years of writing take a toll on her. The trip from Vancouver to San Miguel is doing her in.

In this Fabulous Turquoise House

Elspeth rented in San Miguel, she finally has a desk as long as Nicole Brossard's. There's plenty of room for her resources and friends' books. Sun rays pierce a couple of rafters overhead.

Thoughts, like tiny arrows, fly through her head more quickly than her wee fingers can move on the keyboard, where she cobbles out a ten-finger prelude. She thinks of the cantina down the street, opening right about now. In the old days, she could blast down there for one quick shot of tequila, chat up the ex-pats. She says to herself as her Aunt Flo the poet would say, riffing on an e.e. cummings "How shall we fill this most amazing day?" She reaches over to her night table, glances at her blackberry: gym, writing, lunch with Marion.

The guttural "readle-eek" of a grackle, like the opening of a rusty gate, reminds her of where she is. She is volunteering to teach creative writing at Casa Hogar Santa Julia Don Bosco, the girls' orphanage. A truck with a loudspeaker on its roof bumps over brick street stones. "Naranjas!" "Fresas!" on sale at seven a.m. Another fellow with a Santa-sized sack of canned beer on his burro's back shouts "Abarrotes!" She feels the edges of her mouth turn up. Lizard, as her brother would call her, likes this place. Her mother disapproved of her brother calling her Lizzy Lizard, Elspeth liked the nickname Lizzy. *Way hay and up she rises, early in the morning,* she sings.

As she tattoos her eyebrows on in the bathroom mirror, her once feral kitty vies for her attention, David Gray's "As I'm Leaving" plays in the background. She begins to cry. Pharrell's "Happy" dances through her veins. In this moment, listening to this music, everything is coming together and overwhelming her with how wonderful life can be. A single, simple moment.

Settling Into Mexico

A plane overhead. A street dog barks. Lizzy looks down from her clouds. A big rig is winding down the brown hills into the village. The neighbour screams in English "I'm tired of living on top of each other."

Lizzy dreamed of a writer in Vancouver's Chinatown last night. Janit Dawn. Janit introduced her to a bunch of her gay friends and took her to a farm where there were fresh grain-fed chickens and little pigs. The farmer handed her a pig delicately and she says she does the same for the chickens that are having a pleasant gabble there.

She lathers her legs and arms with mosquito spray to beat the night bites and enjoys the sting. She keeps spraying the spot where she has a little cut to feel that titch of pain, again and again. The cat's tongue trills. How can a person twitter the day away in the name of writing and find that she has not written, nor done anything else of value? What does she do with those minutes, hours? She slaps together lunch and crawls into the closet for the afternoon. At Happy Hour though, she gobbles up the sunset. Her mouth is larger than when her mouth guard is in it. With each bite, the sunset grows deeper, darker, more delicious. She is thinking of trying cashews on her spaghetti tonight, the ones Jane Siberry gave her which she found in her pocket.

Lizzy has an obsession with having everything in its right place. As a girl, she knew when her sister had been in her room, looking at her things. She knew how she placed each item on her dresser, the direction each pointed in and if anything had been moved. Even her nails are cut perfectly straight.

Relative Distance: Memories

Lizzy remembers back in Vancouver that she witnessed a fat white man fly, ending a six-floor fall from a balcony of the Abbott Mansion, body bouncing, conk on concrete in the alley of the one hundred block, between Hastings and Pender.

She headed west on Abbott, right up Pender, left to one hundred Beatty, the Sun Tower, once the World Building (home of the *World* newspaper / the *Vancouver Sun*), completed in 1912 for $100,000. Her great Aunt MaryAnn Gillies was the elevator operator (so that's how Mary came to feel at home in the pubs around Hastings and Main. It's not where Liz's mother hung out). Mary from the island of Barra in 1927 worked in this lofty structure, highest in the British Empire, for two years.

Mary, party queen of the wildest cèilidhs danced the Sailor's Hornpipe in glittery gold go-go boots, sixties psychedelic pinks, oranges, sang 'A is for Anchor,' gave Lizzy a quarter for each beer Mary drank, saw the *Sun* through a peppered history of changing names, bankruptcy, mechanics liens and a threat of foreclosure.

On the seventeenth floor, Lizzy opened the bathroom window, ran her fingers over the outside wall, millimeter-wide vertical combed lines. Someone had grained the concrete. Lizzy washed, white chipped corroding enamel of the sink broke off into her palm. Did her aunt touch this place fifty years ago or ever?

Macchiato at the Nine Maidens Cafe at the bottom of the World Building. A businessman with his tie flung over his shoulder, coins falling out of his pockets, glowers at Lizzy every time she pops a bubble. She remembers Mary's story about her gay co-worker, "Mary, my partner and I need to borrow a ballroom dress." They picked their favourite at her home on Adanac. When she asked for it back "Oh I'm so sorry Mary. We had an orgy (She pronounced it with a hard g). It got ripped apart."

The last time Lizzy held Mary's ninety-four year old hand, she was whimpering in pain "How, how, how." After a few minutes, Mary said "You can go now." Lizzy knows Mary meant, "Now I can go."

Atotonilco

Elspeth decides to volunteer at the San Miguel library. They are hosting an all-night pilgrimage from there to Atotonilco. Lizzy brings two of her students, Larizza and Maripaz. They shuffle along with the cortege towards the light. Fire in oil drums, orange and blue flames leap into black night. Racks of T-shirts of Our Lord of the Column beside images of Metallica, the Virgin of Guadalupe, scantily dressed blonde girls with large breasts. Larizza buys herself a small wooden crucifix. Christ's arms are pinned above his embroidered bamboo head, red sequins at his hands and feet, red velvet loin cloth at his waist. Scent of roasted chicken, corn tortillas, the three amble along. The throng of believers wearing ponchos, carrying blankets, and lanterns, past tables with religious items, toys, and pottery.

Blue light overhead, tired looking folks lean against the lucent Church of Atotonilco. Hundreds of the penitent file into the church where the beaten and bloodied statue of Our Lord of the Column waits behind glass. Maripaz weeps as the brothers in short-waisted blue jackets, 'San Juan de Dios Brotherhood,' inspect the body of our Lord. Shine little lights in his eyes, on his bones, pin scarves on him, for the twelve-kilometer pilgrimage to San Miguel. How still the Lord waits.

Inside the church, a woman with a decorative black scarf over her head recites the first half of the Hail Mary. The crowd murmurs the second half, which Lizzy recognizes as the recitation of the rosary. She feels claustrophobic in the church; the smell of these strangers' sweat so close. She taps the girls' shoulders "Let's go." Outside, devotees sit on the ground eating gorditas, roasted corn on the cob, pink cotton candy angel hair. At midnight, parishioners dressed as roman soldiers depart the sanctuary and accompany the procession. People cry as their Lord passes by, pray for a miracle. Larizza asks to kiss Our Lord's foot to fulfill a promise to her dead grandmother. Maripaz warns her it's forbidden.

The next morning at five a.m., the Avenida Independencia, near the town square, is adorned with purple and white balloons, tissue paper flowers, and the new blossoms of fennel and chamomile. Rockets explode, hymns of praise are sung; the statue of Our Lord of the Column is placed on the high altar of the Church of San Juan de Dios. The solemn mass is led by the Bishop of Celaya, a look of mercy in Our Lord's eyes.

All the King's Horses

Lizzy hears herself slurp as her tongue makes contact with her palate. Her breath oceanic air in a conch, she exhales, steams up her glasses. Her hand slides across the blank page as she remembers what it's like to handwrite. The Apple people are erasing her hard drive deleting her current programs. Pages merge and disappear. She only wishes her recovery process was as simple, erasing her desire to evade reality.

She strings strange sentences in her mouth, hears the nasal click of her jaw, saliva tickling the edges of her lips, while more words twist and coil. Sometimes her eyes closed, blepharospasm ensues. She blinks hard and cannot stop blinking. Her eyelids clamp shut, like having myasthenia gravis.

"All the King's horses and all the King's men," cannot put Elspeth together again.

emily and Elspeth

gonna sex your cherry

emily cannot bend her legs   tires protrude
beneath her bus seat   she tires of the same old super happy
boppy poppy loco tunes blaring

       on the buses in San Miguel   hums her dirty little ditty
                in her hot-wired head

     "o cutie pie, apple of my eye
     wrap your legs round my waiting thigh
     gonna sex your cherry   gonna wanna marry
     my cutie pie"

blossoms periwinkle from jacaranda outside
the bus window   float by emily's float-by eyes down

down and scattered   on Calle Salida
              someone has turned on the sun
clouds   swallows   the sky azure sure

pearl of sweat on emily's nose   she pours water
into her left palm   tosses it onto her right shoulder
     right palm   left shoulder   water dribbles down

her neck   and her spine   from manubrium to laparoscopic belly
scars   her belly button   and pools   over her pancake belly bowl
    down the thin line of coarse black hair gathering

at the edge of panties   cooling her crotch   trickles through her
         ordinary body of joy   the bus at standstill by
Farmacia Guadalajara and there under the palm

 emily sees a woman in jean cut offs   Burks   a Michigan Woman's
Music Festival tank top   sexy shades   rosy cheeks   dark eyebrows,
silver hoop in nose   tanned   around fifty   ball cap with a

rainbow sign   short dark hair   gotta be a dyke
the woman glances   looks around   bends her head down again

scribbles something   emily wonders *is she too a writer?*

bolsa de garbanzos con chili y lima at her side
                    the bus driver lodges his engine

the fruit man on the shady corner,
straw hat   white shirt   slices jímaca   piña

green melon   watermelon   packs clear plastic
bags full   corn on the cob over a mesquite fire

in an oil drum   bag of chilli powder   limes
and mayo   people perched on stools outside

the taco stands   gobble heuvos con chorizo y queso
in tortillas   tote home wee knotted plastic bags

of salsa verde

Casa Hogar

"oh la paloma blanca"
emily doesn't even like ABBA
why that song now?

yanks on the rope outside the Casa Hogar Santa Julia
orphanage for girls in San Miguel   Catholics gave her the willies
the Madre of her past   body shrouded   tone restrained
emily recalls "No whistling in the hall
after school"

a priest opens the metal gate   his finger-thin moustache
sour taste in emily's mouth
priests with a hankering for girls
gives her the once over like she was a strumpet
in her red cowboy hat   bottleneck
guitar slung over her shoulder   horses on her belt buckle
cowboy shirt   emulating j. cash

his eyes pause
breast level

but this Madre greets emily in a business suit for God
she takes her job very seriously
believes in the direct intervention of the saints
if St. Anthony fails to answer her request
she turns his image upside-down
to punish him

extends a rough tiny hand   her father a shoemaker
Robin the American secretary translates

a hunched over birdchild
twists fists in a fetal position
eyes crossed   rocks forward and back

"this is Alma" twenty-six years old "she loves music"
Robin says "bailemos" Robin takes Alma's curled hands
the two of them dance
Alma's face twists into a kind of joy

girls scurry   casa smells of tile cleaning products
one child waters a giant willow

woman with sorrel eyes approaches Robin

"oh hi Elspeth   Emily this is the gal i've been telling you about"   emily grins
the cinnamoned woman she saw from the bus window yesterday

"this is Elspeth   she is giving a non-fiction workshop on the girls' pilgrimage
to Atotonilco"

lizzy lingers

plastic chairs in the chapel   emily leaves the crowd a moment
gathers herself in the washroom   fights off an ensuing case of Montezuma's
revenge

returns
lizzy's eyes on emily
        emily's nervousness in her amplified presence
emily describes the originals in piecemeal spanglish
Theresa translates   her Spanish impeccable

"i could go down to the tavern
polish off the dregs
but the preacher came and found me
said i'm gonna tan your hide
i'm goin bad
badder 'n i bin before ..."

the priest's eyes grow large

"ready-to-bop-drop-the-rock-acid-groovy-lava-java-
lip-hip-kill-the-pup-let-her-rip-let-her-roll, body-shakin-
head-bangin-fuzzy-technicolour-pop-groan-trip-a-type-A
not-a-sleep-in-the-day-good-bad-blues-kinda-girl"

the girls eat it up
        hoot   whistle   love her harping to the guitar riffs

she tells them they can be anything   do anything

the madre chomps on her nails during emily's performance

lizzy sees
a wee thing of six kisses emily on the cheek
honours her with a gold crucifix
streams of girls now coming up to her
        kisses   hugs
reins back tears

emily and lizzy head down Quebrado
to the market for a bite

blessed are those

emily would like to eat there again
picks a bag of frutas   thinks *blessed*

are those who come in the name of the
Lord   by their fruits   you will know them

the woman running the stand eyes emily
suspiciously   what's she scribbling   head up

scrutinizing   shadow of hand and hat
on her page   bunches of roses and calla

lilies line the concrete wall

knock knock who's there

3 a.m. rooster
4 a.m. church bells
5 a.m. fireworks

emily wants to rip her own face off   hate the day away. she'd asked for descafeina-
do   not a sleepless night   a fly in her nosehair   sand in her mouth   Ba   she
whips off her eye patch undoes her wrist braces   mouth guard   ear plugs   ap-
plies makeup remover

7 a.m. construction workers
8 a.m. lawn mower
9 a.m. the waterman

reclines in the bath   her introverted room   the "be bad tanyas"   two rubescent
roses edge the tub   sound of the great tailed grackle and blessed rain on ocotillo
cactus   her borders settle into lizzy's joke   "get thee to a nunnery"

10 a.m. gorditas de queso
11 a.m. beggar at door
12 p.m. jugo de uva

what a surprising delight meeting mz lizzy yesterday   what shape might they take?
emily hopes lizzy's planet is in her galaxy   that it's not the old case of wanting the
unavailable or discovering that actually

1 p.m. churros in baskets
2 p.m. tamale girl
3 p.m. calla lily lady

emily'll have to use her handy-dandy caretaking skills   wonders what drives lizzy
recalls her ready wit "with your frida bag and your frida blouse   it looks like you're
a frida everything!"   hopes lizzy isn't a frida her

4 p.m. Krishnamurti people
5 p.m. neighbour for piano lesson
6 p.m. hot tortillas de maíz azul

emily hadn't realized how close to the truth lizzy's little taradiddle was   in the
interim   her hot and unsorted parts ache for this naughty hottie

San Miguel Writers' Conference

Lizzy was picking up her latte from the Hotel Mina Real's grand salon bar when she saw Emily from Casa Hogar. Outside the sun baptized the wisteria. Emily had been appearing in her text.

Though she'd just seen her once at the orphanage, she was developing a passion for Emily. Their talk afterwards spurred Lizzy to write at ungodly hours, to unravel the story behind those eyes. She queries the direction in which she and Emily are headed, realizing she's lonely and begins to imagine telling people about meeting Emily and their being together. Lizzy knows she spends too much time daydreaming about potential futures with people that barely acknowledge her or who don't reciprocate the same attention she gives them. She needed to stop trolling for ghosts, yet somehow that evening she knew in her heart something grand waited for her, something real.

There was a time when she was busy manufacturing a most idiotic relationship with death. She planned it inimitably. She'd catch the train in Regina, take a bottle of pills on the last day of travel to Vancouver. Her family would find her emptied out upon arrival. There was nothing holding her to a world bereft of colour. The family motto was "Don't ask, don't tell." She'd never admit to this in a million years. Not even to Emily. Seeing Emily from a distance gives her a thrill. "Another day in paradise." Today, Lizzy wouldn't change a thing.

The racket in the lobby increases, clatter of cups in the polylingual room.
"Hello Elspeth" Emily says from behind a holly bush.
Lizzy blushes, carmine like the berries, looks up.
"Why Emily. What a pleasant surprise." Lizzy shuffles the conference papers that her head is buried in. "You can call me Lizzy. What are you doing here?"
"I'm here for the Writer's Conference."
"So am I! How lovely! Do you want to head over? The keynote speaker starts any time now."
"Let me help you Lizzy" says Emily grabbing some of Lizzy's books. The two women saunter towards the ballroom. Lizzy sees the face of her twin in the glass beside the walkway.

chiclets, chachalaca and chocolate

the flowerboy awaits a sale   his baby
hair tight in pigtails   sucks on rocks

a boy of six   left eye superating
approaches emily to sell her Carlos V

candy bars   and chiclets   a rickshaw
passes by with the sign "Rentame"

chachalaca screech   emily grabs
her chatchkas and chocolate

hops aboard the bus

Tuckems

Lizzy doesn't regret having slept on Emily's couch the day they met at the Writers' Conference. It was only a matter of time. It turned out that Emily lived on Quebrado near the Bellas Artes where the two had dined and laughed for hours. It got so late in fact, that Emily suggested that Lizzy sleep on her couch.

Lizzy had been intrigued with Emily since the first time she saw her under the palm by Farmacia Guadalajara, scribbling. The poet, ready for anything, plopped down on her bottom. Over dinner, they discovered that they were both from the west coast of Canada, Lizzy from the mainland, Emily from Victoria. They knew women in common, women each other had had relationships with or just slept with. They spent a little too much time talking and getting to know each other for their first visit. When just getting to know someone, Lizzy generally didn't spend more than an hour or two with them at first but it was refreshing to find a like-minded soul that spoke the same language. They had that "Perhaps I knew you in another life" feeling. They had read the same books as youngsters, Enid Blytons' *The Circus of Adventure, The Island of Adventure, Nobody's Girl* and *Nobody's Boy* and *Marjorie Morningstar.* They'd needed to be thrown into worlds that would carry them away. Both had an absent parent and looked after one of their parents.

Lizzy came out at twenty, living with a woman ten years her senior, who was married. This woman would go home after university, greet the kids home from school, cook supper, and then return to her other home with Lizzy to go to sleep.

Emily, having been a Catholic school teacher, came out when she was thirty. The other teachers called her a lesbian. How could they tell? She did everything in her power to hide it. The male teachers would take her to strip bars and give her and her sisters cocaine. She led a double life and kept her sexuality in the closet, thinking it would devastate her parents and jeopardize her job. It could have. There was a gay Catholic school teacher who at that time in Vancouver in the early eighties was let go because he was found to be living 'in sin' with another man.

Lizzy felt immediately comfortable and so nurtured when Emily brought her a big fleece blanket and tucked her in on the couch. She bent over Lizzy and pushed the blanket in around her torso, her legs, even her feet, giving her affectionate touches. As she manoeuvred the blanket around Lizzy, she said "Tuckems, Tuckems." Emily's dad used to do this. Lizzy got a big kick out of it. Just before Emily said goodnight, she kissed her hand and laid that kiss on Lizzy's cheek. Then Emily's cat curled up on top of Lizzy's belly. She dreamt of galloping on white horses on a long white sandy beach, the sun blazing gleefully.

all of San Miguel

why wait?
close the windows

shut the curtains
amor is trapped in her casa

fire in her bedroom
ignites her kitchen

all of San Miguel
streetlocked in fire

mouth unsealed
under tongue

her multi-coloured huipil around her ears
her body an earthquake

held breath   explodes
          the earth opens up

trap-door to the sky

cuni

          cuni

                    cuni

Heading Home: Hand in Hand

Lizzy and Emily wait on Calle de Salida for a cab at 4:30 a.m. Bird song on the deliriously delicious morning of their leave-taking of San Miguel de Allende. "I wish I felt that way in the morning" she tells Emily.

They're freezing in the dark desert air and Emily blurts out "I've got chills, They're multiplying and I'm losing control." Lizzy slaps Emily's bum. "Where in the hell is that cabbie?"

Lizzy runs back into the casa and calls the combi but no answer. San Miguel is asleep. She's worried they may miss their flight until she remembers the number of another cabbie, Marco. She calls and he flies over. The women are aghast as he burns down the dusty two-lane highway, in what may have been a '69 Toyota. Lizzy squeezes Emily's hand so hard, not a lot of blood is left running in it. Elspeth is useless in chaos.

Emily babbles to Marco in Spanish. Questions come easily. She's genuinely interested in everyone, can enter anybody's head in a flash. Strangers open to her spontaneously. It's a rare gift she told Lizzy from her mother. Marco longs to send his eldest daughter to university. So, Lizzy is attempting to jot down his bank information as he guns it to the airport.

They have seven bags between the two of them including the cat Emily found wandering about her neighbourhood. And of course there are Lizzy's hats, lime green and navy, which remind Emily of 'the curse.' That was the wicker picnic basket that her dad used to try to shove into their station wagon. He couldn't jam the damn thing into the car without swearing a lot. He'd drive with the back window open, the handle hanging out. The gaggle of McMahons were squished in the back section with the water toys.

Emily's in the aisle seat cuz she often has to pee. Lizzy sits in the middle seat beside a heavy white business-like fellow. He has taken over her armrest. Their plane is whipped by whopping winds. Emily holds Lizzy 'til it settles down. Lizzy's not the religious type, but she'll say a few prayers in times like these.

The Gravol helps her to relax and sleep most of the way back to Vancouver. Now this is going home. She leans lazily into Emily, her eyelids shut, her head against Emily's; hand in hand.

Kiss Me Hardy

Lizzy is over the moon to show Emily the home she's building. Emily hasn't been up to the upper Sunshine Coast since she and her sister rode up from Aunty T's in Halfmoon Bay in the seventies. They were leaving for four months so they had to schlep a whole load of shite. Emily had a piano keyboard, guitars, a banjo, mandolin, accordion, music books, amplifiers. They dragged scuba gear, fishing poles, life jackets, marine gas, water, groceries, clothing, books, and computers, down the steep dock and into the zodiac.

Once on the sea, the girls glory bound like panting dogs, bounce over white caps. Their tongues hang out. "How many seas can a white dove sail" they belt out as they shazam across the mensch. They breathe in turquoise waves to the island they call 'Kiss Me Hardy' - Hardy's last words to Lord Nelson.

Countless boxes and bags into the wheelbarrow, up the steep, shiny, black dock, under the kingfisher's nest. They settle into fat honeyed days, swollen with desire. Lizzy takes Emily's slender body by night.

The two float in the bathwater bay beside Sometimes Island, Lizzy's silken thighs between Emily's. Their bodies weightless. Separate. Lizzy could die of too much pleasure, the feel of their naked bodies wrapped in the bounty of each other's arms. Before ferns, mossy glens, beneath raven cry in the cedar sunset air. And by eve, Lizzy's cheeks, royal flush before the flames. Hearts full, under blanket.

man with a cam

emily points her tapered nose up the coast
a tourist with a camera keeps his distance

she squirts OFF! on   talks back
to the audacious sun
   under the featureless sky
      shut for business

washes sea asparagus and what-cha-ma-call-its
with arsenic water
   bites her lip

life   a high-stake game
suicidal crickets collide in the rackety wind
lizzy wondered   then asked why that man with the cam
was in the marina

the disappearing slug
washes the clutter off her body
jumps into her insected maryjanes

      self-fabulizes

                  on the tramp

pump it   pump it   pump it

be good body

emily dawdles on the rabbit-pelleted-deer-rutted-path
dawn cracks out of the corner of her unassisted eye
admits light to the interior
back flashes black raven

standing emily engages her diaphragm
the mouth open   throat roll
          a glottal thrill   "rrah rrah"

startled "ah" a-ware
      raven flips
right side up to up side down
back again   five flips   six

chipmunks rabbit on   turn tail
their trill shrill for peach
more moldy rasps
berries

outside the inside out house emily
picks pine needles out of her keyboard
pens turn to
syringes

her be good body
  B12
the Be Good Tanyas
be good
for goodness sake

moon strokes

the earplugs emily removes drown
the sound of mice   descent of alder leaves flaxen

the man with the cam   dreamchaser

seagull squall on Hardy   summer
       salt
sitting on rigs   creosote   riprap

watching a deer swim to   Sometimes Island
wants to be back in the arbutus-eating-peanut-butter-jelly
sandwiches like Lady Mary Wortley

instead she hurls off the duvet   jogs the diagnosis away
humans get up her nose   pop out
even the starlings show off

somersault like bombers   the sun   so demanding
                       so cock of the walk

bleaches the world   conformity   hard to care
recoiling into something   massages

bi-est on her face   pats her numb plum tum
We *didn't cut through muscle*
It was just soft tissue

that soft tissue will not keep her on the couch

the soft tissue keeps her on the couch by day by night

that soft tissue pleasures lizzy's hands   her
flat fingers flow   moon strokes over the contours of emily's back
slither down   to the tips   of her beloved's toes

emily awakens

to a letter in her mailbox
she is excited to receive mail
it arrives so rarely
she reads

Dec. 20, 2010

British Columbia XXXXXXXX XXXXXXXXXX
372-1042 Pleasant Valley Road,
Vernon, BC
V5Z 4P2

Dear Emily McMahon,

The law requires that we review your case from time to time to verify that you are still disabled. We require you to attend a special examination. You will be notified in writing.

Your disability payments will stop immediately if at the examination, it is determined that you no longer have a disability.

If you have more than one disabling condition, we will consider the combined effects of all your impairments on your ability to work. Should your medical condition have improved and we decide you can work, your disability payments will discontinue.

Thank you,

H. Gaudette
Income Security
XXXXXXXXX School Board

it dawns on emily
the man with the cam is hired by the Sun Life
is the culprit she sees following her around
is the one with the camera in the suite across the street
faced square into her living room
that surveils her every move
sees things that should not be seen
sees her stretch   vacuum
and she loves
her couch

popping back to vancouver

emily dreams wanted food particles swim into her bloodstream
poems fall out of her ears   the one about meeting Spiderman

in The Louvre   emily returns to lizzy for the first time in Vancouver's
West End   em's body fits into lizzy's   Her naked behind tucked into

lizzy's stomach   emily's arm draped over her belly   emily needs
lizzy to continue being so wonderful   groggy groggy   this sun-keen

morning lizzy awakens with a "where am i?" debussy's "afternoon
of the fawns" in earreach   "oh i just feel like chirping" as if the

swallows outside the bedroom window wanted a contralto

love is patient, love is kind
love is a cup of coffee on time

emily on the lip of the bed hands lizzy a steaming latte,   sticks her finger
in it as she inimitably does   places a smackeroo   top of her noggin

"ooh your hair smells like hair" "you think you can get away
with anything when i laugh at you" says lizzy with the kind kind of eyes

that hug   takes everything in clearly in one glance   through her new
tri-focals   draws em's lips towards her   "take my tongue anytime

then i'll be speechless" lizzy says   crawls onto the bed   the two kiss their sweet
lives hello   between ebullient banjo blues   between syllables and thighs

phosphorescent rings pulse in third eyes   oo la la   goodness will surely
follow them all of their lives   let us give thanks   "my love she lays me

down on Stó:lō land" every move on earth a prayer   and a struggle
freighters aground in Stanley Park   six year old girl with a padded bra

a Davie Street strumpet   homeless girl in a sleeping bag at the bus stop
at Burrard and Davie covers her face with cardboard   pigeonscream

under wheels on Nelson   still emily expects something good to happen
her tongue untied   no worries at all at all   no one follows anyone

mechanical tin cans don't crash into each other to feel   no crackups
since she began showing lizzy her world   on the good red road   she

boogies over bridges   laughs good-bye to gephyrophobic days   no
scamps with cams on her tail   as her plump heart pumps   the ear

empties   "if i put my ears against yours   will i hear the wind again?"

look at where we are

brrrring brrrring
the room fills up with emily's voice   her jubilance
"like your principles   call you back   we're just sitting down
for our apple-banana-carrot-beet-ginger-juice"
tenderness toward the caller
deer on the terrace guttling down organic kale from lizzy's hands
Isis in fine form grimaces at this belly-god looking deeply into her eyes

emily slippers by   sees the night light in a box of gifts for lizzy's niece
calls back last night's love making
dancing on plexi-glass   loose-limbed
acquiescing to the other's rhythm
the slope of her ribs   jut of her hips
her cry lifting over the strait

treetops explode   sparklers
elders shift   circle
as above   so below
in the sky   in the earth
squirrels dash out on branches, mouths
full of nuts   birds
peck peck pecking on the windowsill
happy as the dickens

"look at where we are"
"how long can this last?" emily shouts

"for the rest of our lives" lizzy cheers

two mouth-guarded "hot-flashing" girls
lizzy and emily bedded   raining over the other   hug
in a puddle   any hotter they'd expire

Ecstatic Risky Business

Lizzy kisses her love, the air staccatoed with strident trochee. It is she, at home with these contours. Her crotch pulsing. An ecstatic slide in a sunless world when spring bursts. This throbbing elating, the angle on which she rides Emily's legs. The wet in creases. Fingers hoisted like wings into timelessness. She thinks there should be a blossom throbbing through her head, replays the ecstatic risky business.

The Closest Place to Heaven

Lizzy's mother, a game gal from Greenwood, good on her pins and always
on the get go, flies into Comox in the silk underwear she hunts in,

ferries over to the Sunshine Coast, where Emily, the social emissary
greets her with a grand bouquet, dahlias of indigo and peach.

Lizzy, big grin, mouthful of bleached teeth, squeezes Evelyn, her mother, tight.
Emily takes notes for the Great Canadian poem. Evelyn chunters on about

card games and golf and who wants her this's and that's, the Duncan Phyfe,
the Chip and Dale's. "I'm closer to the throne but further from the links"

Lizzy says, itching for her mother's clubs. The girls find themselves behind
a hand of gin rummy. Continues "Breast your cards cuz you're not playing
with a full deck"

"And your elevator doesn't go to the top" Emily quips.

"It's too late my dear. God's gonna get you for that" says Lizzy holding aces
"and besides you've lost your fiddle."

"Who are you to talk?" Emily inquires.

Lizzy again "You're sittin' there with a loaf of bread under each arm while
holy doodle, I'm shooting myself in the noodle."

"It's your turn." "Emily's is in bunches like bananas." Lizzy's turn. Turning trump.
Emily surges with her devil's luck. Hot flashes in front of the fire, jumps on Lizzy,

takes her down with her left leg. Lizzy wallops Emily who whops her back
the two cats fight. Emily fires cards at Lizzy's noggin. Cards that pierce the air

Evelyn addlepated, chuckles at the girls' shenanigans, takes a drink of
nonsense, starts down the flooded gutter.

Snivels "I'm afraid I'll never be back here again, Elspeth. I better soft shoe outa'
here to get some shuteye before the whole kit and kaboodle arrive tomorrow.
Toodaloo."

Emily hears her Stratocaster calling her to "Channel Janice"
pauses to read what her mother has written in the guest book:

Bud often said that our condo was the closest place to Heaven he would ever get. This
would be right up there with it. Thank you for showing me such a fabulous time.
Love Mom xoxo

Evelyn gives the girls a box of chocolates, "Laura Secord" heroine
of the war of 1812 when Canadian forces defeated American troops,

tells Elspeth that she's so glad Emily has found her.

a promise ring

emily calls elspeth to vast things
             i am so afraid to love you

open is you
              open am i

emily washes lizzy's hair over the outdoor kitchen sink
strong nails massaging her scalp long after her hair is clean

in the afternoon lizzy motors off to Hummingbird Cove
emily waves from the dock   pays out the chain

even the air has wishes for her return
there are stars in the sea and a second sun

emily is a tree melting with light
lizzy her roots

emily's tossed into sky

lines of light criss-cross through her   fan out like brushfire

they have no bodies   mouths full of stars
make astral shapes
needles and leaves in emily's hair

emily lies down on their bed
stretches her long limbs
eyes on the ceiling of their island home and the words
       you may never live in a house again
you may never see that man with the cam again

eyes shut
faces drift towards her
the one she loves walks in the room

emily falls asleep first
part of her sleeps inside lizzy
she exhales   warm air over lizzy's face

awakens to find a short strand of lizzy's hair on her flannel pillowcase
threads the strand   a promise ring 'round her fourth finger

it is all here

a thousand things must happen for something to once come right

emily carries lizzy with her   returns to her as if for the first time

a scary day for bodies
careful statements of commitment
gathering disparate selves   other half of their heart beats

her beloved fills the birdhouse with
seed   tilts solar panels towards the
sun   writes "you love me" on her thigh

let us hie homeward within

last night when lizzy came   she flew up into trees
spilled into sky   headfull of falling stars   emily thought
she lost her as she ascended

sang   "it is all here
no need to throw one's eyes into the heavens"

something ignites

two women   warm flesh of one around the other   asleep   how then
comes the impulse to open eyes? four a.m.   "Fire!" emily shrieks   "the woods
are on fire!"   four feet high and wide   seventy feet from the bower   bowl
of water   a kettleful   in the event of fire   an extinguisher   point to base

of flame   pull trigger   the fire unchanged   emily and lizzy   a brigade   hose
forty-steps from the flames   containers   wash buckets   wheelbarrow   push
uphill   smoke   smoldered   slope-shouldered   "sparks here"   "more flames
here   "we can't do this alone"   lizzy calls 911   "could the emergency wait

til morning?"   emily calls 411   water slosh   spit   ssss   embers everywhere
"Hardy Island"   Lot three across from Saltery Bay   one thought   one body
lizzy   limb of strength   fireman's flashlight   sparks   pancake over pulpy soil
berry drupelets   necrotic stumps   root rot burns   no name or number of

"Mr.Go-to-Work" lizzy stands topless   ground sizzle   teethes   spits   steam
under soles   burning bush   haul water   soak the smoke   everything to purpose
what if the water runs out?   "they're mobilizing a crew from Comox"   miracle
of first light   fire seventy-five feet in diameter   Mr.Go-to-Work

pulses past them in his boat   the operator says "go to the farthest point of
land   take whatever lights you have   wave them in the air"   helicopter circles
Talking Bay   run to the rocks   switch to yellow boat coats   waving banners
in arcs of half circles   orange lights   their hope   a violent sucking

of wind right above them   "they want us to get away" lizzy hollers   rotor blades
of the Long Ranger III   running to higher ground   lizzy's shawl whips 'round
their heads like a wedding veil   blades wicked the air   a fireman lifts a clot
of moss   his hand in the charred earth up to wrists   looks for hot spots

"we cold trail for fire holding over   can take a hundred years before it ignites"
six lengths of fifty-foot hose   pump at the foreshore   Ministry camera
shots   the good forest   the good island   lizzy couldn't close her eyes in bed that
night   fires beneath it   beneath them   "put you head on my shoulder" emily urged

lizzy's body massive   her muscles huge   blue   bursting   "i can't protect you here"
she cried   "but you woke up elspeth"

a perfect sail

because   emily awakens happier today than is warranted

because   lizzy's lemonyellow tulips grow up her blinds
          blend, bend and bow in evelyn's vase
          arms in first position

because   she has seen how lizzy makes a picture
          felt her hands upon her shy feet
          full of stories

because   she has felt lizzy's warm breath upon her cheek
          tasted her tongue wrapped 'round her own
          lizzy's moan in her left ear

because   she breathes her words
          feels them settle
          lizzy's hand on her belly

when she goes to the moon tonight
she wishes from her western shore
to open like a perfect sail

Coda

True Love Has Been Returned to Me

Lizzy lives on Hardy as much as she can, in fair weather. She has a new lover who lives on the east side of Canada, which suits her well, the shape of their romance created through absence. When in Vancouver, they eat at the best restaurants or order in, now that the world is beset by a pandemic. They sleep in 400 thread count sheets in Lizzy's home over the ocean in False Creek.

Yesterday she and her lover swam in the bay out front on Hardy Island, naked. The water, warmed by the sun all day, deliciously enveloped them, her new lover's long, strong legs around her. Hugging, floating, the softness of their flesh comingling. Oh unimagined joy of life, sky and homeland in their arms and legs.

Tonight Lizzy sits in her bathtub, hot water up to her neck, peers through the glass floor, at her lover curled up on the rug in front of the fire, reading her last book Bring Me One of Everything. Lizzy looks out at the heart-filled sky over Sometimes Island, Maria Callas sings Casta Diva from Norma, thinks This is my life. My one 'shot at the divine.' True love has been returned to me and I will protect her against the whole world. Hope has taken wing. Victory.

rainbird

emily rainbirds in Apache Junction   Arizona
at the lesbian trailer park

every fall she shazams in the van with dog
cat   musical instruments   her spices

it just so happens that there is a grand piano
in the ballroom across from her trailer

and she has made level two in the tennis club
club   she and the ukulele ladies jam in her carport

on Tuesdays and Thursdays   on Mondays and
Wednesdays   she plays in the blues band

in the music studio   every morning she goes
to free yoga classes and rides her bike around

the trailer court   her dog in tow   panting away
after her smoothie of papaya   mango   pomegranate

from Thurza's tree   she swims fifteen laps in the
warm pool   closes her eyes under sunhat on the

chaise lounge breathes deeply in and out   allows her
belly to fully extend   in the pool, on a noodle

she chats up the other noodle floaters   at night
the lesbians' laughter rises like helium balloons

they cozy up naked in the hot tub   tell stories ·
of who came out when and where   they get a rise

out of emily   the flying nun   who taught in the Catholic
schools   getting high by night   called a lesbian by the

Christian brothers by day   now she kayaks in Canyon Lake
glides up to the richest rock fest on the isthmus   hoards

purple quartz   ant-hill garnet   blesses the earth   when she
gets bored   she pops down to Nashville to write songs

drives into Mexico to feel at home again   flies over to Africa
to sing with Ethiopian kids   of course   she loves her couch still

her siestas   meditation and films   takes nothing for granted
having been born into this undeserved life of entitlement

from nowhere to now here finally

says "ho'oponopono"   looks back on her life with Elspeth   we all
leave a piece of our hearts in the other and that   lovelies   is enough

home to her

the gals went their separate ways ten years ago
just before emily's fiftieth birthday

they didn't see eye to eye   had differing views
of the future   earth and water don't mix

still for emily their parting was achingly heart rending
she picked her belongings up at her twin's house

they could no longer face one another   the last few times
emily saw lizzy   lizzy was wearing her sunglasses

she only saw her one more time a few years after their breakup
at the Vancouver Writer's Festival   lizzy said "i have a new partner now"

a love like that happens but once in a lifetime
the distance between them remains close

although lizzy crossed over recently
one of the millions of souls lost during the pandemic

in the light at the end of the tunnel   lizzy says   "All my life I was a bride
married to amazement   I was the bridegroom   taking the world into my arms

When it is over   I don't want to wonder If I have made of my life something
particular and real … I don't want to end up simply having visited this world"

she took the world and emily into her arms   boundlessly
emily remembers how when lizzy was writing and got stumped

she'd close her eyes before her computer   ask for the right words
and wait   emily stops typing   closes her eyes   takes a deep breath

remembers how in bed lizzy would reach over the ridge of her body
grab her hand and take her arm   one body surrounding the other

the reaching across the divide of their two countries
travelling safely   in sleep

together

Notes to Text

1. code of no go
"ochre time" Nicole Brossard, *Museum of Bone and Water*

2. code of no go
song lyrics from Catherine McNeil's *Let Us Give Thanks*

3. man with a cam in a red sedan
ME and CFS are Myalgic Encephomyelitis and Chronic Fatigue Syndrome is a symptom known as post-exertional malaise which can include problems with sleep, thinking and concentrating, and pain

Some of these lyrics are from Lynne Dickson's song "Ukulele Ladies" which was originally Robert Johnsons' "They're Red Hot"

4. Relative Distant Memories from Vancouver
Some of the information in this poem comes from *The Vancouver Book*, by Chuck Davis

Cèilidh – Gaelic for a social gathering

5. the closest place to heaven
Stratocaster – a Fender electric guitar

6. in to the heavens
"thousand things must happen for something to once come right" Rainer Maria Rilke, *Letters to a Young Poet*

"let us hie homeward within" Paramahansa Yogananda, chant

7. Something Ignites
The "bower" is a cottage beside the main house

8. HO'OPONOPONO
An ancient Hawaiian mantra : I am sorry
                                        Please forgive me
                                        I love you
                                        Thank you

9. home to her
From the Mary Oliver poem "When Death Comes" quoted in the obituary of Leslie Hall Pinder

Appendix

p21. casa: house
siéntete: sit
escúchame: listen to me

p23. esta mañana: this morning

p26. policía: police

p29. huipil : a common traditional garment worn by indigenous women from
Central Mexico to Central America

p30. te gustaría algo?: would you like something?
cuánto cuesta?: how much does this cost?
es gratis: it's free
esposo: husband

p31. corrida de toros: bullfight
banderilleros: a bullfighter who plants the banderillas
bandillera: pole with a metal point decorated with little colourful flags

p35. naranjas: oranges
fresas: strawberries
abarottes: groceries

p43. bolsa de garbanzos con chili y lima: bag of garbanzo beans with chilli and lime
jímaca: the crisp white-fleshed tuber of the yam bean
heuvos: eggs
queso: cheese

p44. bailemos: let's dance

p47. frutas: fruits

p48. gorditas de queso: a dish made with masa and stuffed with cheese
jugo de uva: grape juice
descafeinado: decaffeinated
maíz azul: blue corn

p50. chachalaca: a galliform bird that is social, noisy and common in Mexico

Acknowledgements

these poems were written on the unceded lands of the Musqueam, Tsleil-Waututh and Skwxwú7mesh people.

endless thanks to the team at Caitlin Press: Vici Johnstone, Sarah Corsie and Malaika Aleba and also to editor Yvonne Blomer, whose perspicacious editorial insight into *Emily and Elspeth* has been extraordinary.

infinite and heartfelt gratitude to Betsy Warland, my first and last editor, who has seen into *Emily and Elspeth* with her genius eye and tremendous attention to detail, as well as to Oana Avasilichioaei for resurrecting the manuscript and helping me to see character and to Jami Macarty's keen editorial eye.

a special thanks to Diane McIntosh for her expedient and beautiful work on the cover design of the book, and also thanks to the cover artist RoseAnn Janzen, whose work I have adored for years.

thanks to my first reader and best friend Janit Bianic and Jan Legault, for interesting input in making final decisions.

some of these poems appeared in *Rampike* and *Chroma: A Queer Literary Journal* and *Sinister Wisdom*.

gratitude to my parents Maureen and Alex, who to my great fortune are still alive and supportive of my writing, whose voices you may hear within the characters and to my Aunt Florence McNeil, who wrote seventeen books and showed me I too could be a writer.

lastly to Leslie Hall Pinder without whose love, this book would cease to be.

PHOTO BELLE ANCELL

About the Author

Catherine McNeil is a singer-songwriter multi-instrumentalist whose work has appeared in journals in England, the United States and Canada. Her first book, *under the influence*, won the national contest, Milieu Emerging Writer's Award. She rainbirded between Apache Junction, Arizona or Mexico for half the year and Vancouver, BC before the pandemic. Now she lives peacefully in the seaside town of Gibsons Landing with her dog, Gaia and cat, Lavender. She holds a BA in English from Simon Fraser University, Teacher's Certificate and Diploma in the Deaf and Hard of Hearing from UBC, was a Teacher of the Deaf for the Vancouver School Board. Now retired, she plays in various bands. Her writing and music can be found on catmacmusic.com.